13.07.97

Love,

Charlie

& Jiff

Just a little
something!!

A
GARTER
ROUND THE
BEDPOST

Ladies beware! If a gentleman's arm trembles when you first place your own within it as you take a walk together, watch his conduct towards you narrowly; his love vows will be frail and his promises will easily be broken!

A
GARTER
ROUND THE
BEDPOST

TRADITIONAL LOVE CHARMS
AND SUPERSTITIONS

COMPILED BY J. BARNES

Copper Beech Publishing

Published in Great Britain 1995 by
Copper Beech Publishing Ltd
© Copyright J Barnes 1995
All rights reserved.

ISBN 1-898617-03-1

A CIP catalogue record for this book is available
from the British Library.

Additional research by Beryl Peters

Copper Beech Publishing Ltd
P O Box 159, East Grinstead
Sussex RH19 4FS England

Not only in the springtime
of life does one's fancy
'lightly turn to thoughts of love' - and
in days long ago, many an innocent
device was resorted to by young
women and men to obtain the
desired glimpse of their
future spouse.
Some of these quaint love charms
and superstitions are here recalled
and may afford some amusement by
their recital.

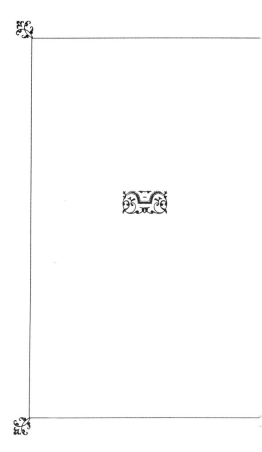

The Food of Love

Every young woman in each household
should help to stir the Christmas
pudding...

Have a care if you carry a nutmeg in
your pocket...

APPLE PEEL

Take an apple, peel it whole, and take
the paring in your right hand and say:
"St Simon and St Jude
On you I intrude
By this paring I hold to discover
Without any delay
To tell me this day.
The first letter of my true-lover."

Turn around three times and cast the
paring over your left shoulder, and it will
form the first letter of your future
husband's name.

WHO WILL YOUR SWEETHEART BE?

Take a summer apple of the best fruit,
stick pins close into the apple to the
head, and as you stick them, take notice
of which of them is the middlemost, and
give it what name you fancy, put it into
thy left glove, and lay it under thy pillow
on Saturday night when thou gettest
into bed, then clasp thy hands together
and say these words:
  "If thou be he that must have me
    To be thy wedded bride
  Make no delay but come away,
    This night to my bedside."

COUNTING THE PIPS

When an apple is eaten to the core count
the pips with this incantation;

One, I love
Two, I love
Three, I love, I say;
Four, I love with all my heart,
Five, I cast away.
Six, he loves,
Seven, she loves
Eight, they both love,
Nine, he comes.
Ten, he tarries,
Eleven, he courts
Twelve, he marries.

The one which goes with the final
number of seeds is the one which
determines the character of the fortune.

APPLE STALK

A girl can discover who she will marry
by twisting the stalk of an apple and
going through the alphabet, a letter for
each twist. The letter she has reached
when the stalk comes off is the initial of
the first name of the man she will marry.
To find the initial of his second name
she taps the apple with the stalk, going
through the alphabet until the stalk
pierces the skin of the apple.

APPLE SEED
Place an apple seed in the palm of the
left hand and cover it with the right,
meanwhile shaking both hands up and
down ...
repeating:
"Kernel, kernel of the apple tree
Tell me where my true love be;
East, west, north or south,
Pretty kernel tell the truth."
Then examine the kernel, and whichever
way the pointed end is found, from that
direction the true love will come.

~

Another apple seed charm; shoot an
apple pip from between the thumb and
the forefinger, saying:

'Kernel, come kernel, hop over my

thumb
And tell me which way my truelove will
come,
East west, north or south
Kernel jump into my truelove's mouth.'

APPLE PIPS (BURNING)

I remember throwing apple pips into the
fire, saying
"If you love me pop and fly,
If you hate me, lay and die."
Think of some individual whose affec-
tion you desire to test.

The maiden takes an apple pip and
naming one of her followers, puts the
pip in the fire. If it makes a noise in
bursting from the heat, it is a proof of
love; but if it is consumed without a
crack, she is fully satisfied that the
person named has no
real regard for her.

The Apple and the Looking Glass

Take a candle and go alone to the looking glass; eat an apple before it; and some say you should comb your hair all the time; the face of your future husband will be seen in the glass, as if peeping over your shoulder.

The Wish of your Heart

Get an apple and slice it in two with a sharp knife.

If you can do this without cutting a seed, the wish of your heart will be fulfilled, but should you cut into the seeds, you will not gain the love of the person.

PIPPINS ON THE TONGS

Place two pippins on the mouth of a pair
of tongs, so as to touch each other. The
lady gives her own name to the left hand
pippin and that on the right must bear
the name of the person whose intentions
are being tested. The tongs must now
be placed in the hollow part of the fire
and if both pippins fly off in the same
direction, the parties will be married: if
on opposite sides, there will be no
union; and if both burn together
without flying off, the gentleman will
never propose.

Names in Bread

Write the initials of six young men of
your acquaintance on six pieces of paper;
in each paper wrap a bit of bread
pinched into a soft mass. Put the six
packets in a glass of water, and he whose
name first rises to the surface will be the
successful suitor.

BREAD AND CHEESE -
(said to be a Russian Charm)
At midnight an unmarried girl, fasting,
lays a cloth upon the table and places
bread and cheese upon it, then, leaving
the outer door ajar, sits down as if to eat
and the ghostly visitant who is supposed
to come and join her will be her future
husband.

BREAD - CUTTING OR PRICKING
Always mark bread with a skewer, not a
knife, for:-
She that pricks bread with a fork or knife
Will never be happy, maid or wife.

CORN IN THE CIRCLE
A large circle should be drawn on a smooth floor, and sufficient radii drawn from the centre of the circle to the circumference to divide it into twenty-four compartments, one for each letter of the alphabet. Next a grain of corn was laid over each of these letters then a cock bird is let in. The grains (or letters) he selected to eat were supposed to spell the initials or name of the future husband or wife.

CABBAGE STALK
Cabbages were torn up from the roots by boys and girls blindfolded, about the hour of midnight. Their heads and stalks were supposed to indicate the physical and mental peculiarities, tidiness, slovenliness etc. of their future spouse.

THE FLOWER OF THE WELL

The instant the clock has struck the midnight hour, one of the family goes to the well as quickly as possible, and carefully skims it .... this 'flower of the well'  signifies the first pail of water, and the girl who is so fortunate as to obtain the prize, is supposed to have more than a double chance of obtaining the most accomplished young man in the parish.

WEDDING-CAKE

Take a small piece of wedding-cake, pass
it three times through a wedding-ring
and lay the cake under your pillow. In
your dreams that night your future
husband will appear to you.

CHRISTMAS PUDDING

Every young woman in each household
should help to stir the Christmas
pudding if she has any wish to be
married during the ensuing twelve
months.

DUMB CAKE

Girls bake the dumb-cake which is made
of the following ingredients:
An egg-shell full of salt
An egg-shell full of wheat meal
An egg-shell full of barley meal
The maker must be quite alone, must be
fasting and not a word must be spoken.
At twelve o'clock exactly the sweetheart
will come in and turn the cake. The
door must be left open.

A Wedding Ring or a Sixpence

At the time of a wedding, make a common flat cake of flour, water, currants, etc and put therein a wedding ring and a sixpence. When the company is able to retire on the wedding day, the cake must be broken and distributed amongst the unmarried females. She who gets the ring in her portion of the cake will shortly be married and the one who gets the sixpence will die an old maid.

Dreaming Bread

Cakes of shortbread are broken over a bride's head, and distributed among the spectators. This is most anxiously sought after, and, if the company is large, it is a peculiar favour to obtain the smallest crumb of this cake, which is known by the name of dreaming bread. When placed below the pillow, the dreamer will see a vision of their future partner for life.

GROANING CHEESE

A large Cheshire cheese, provided on the same occasion as the Groaning cake (an allusion to the mother's groaning and complaints at childbirth and delivery). A slice of the first cut is laid under the pillow of young damsels to enable them to dream of their lovers. It must be pierced with three pins taken from the child's pincushion.

THE CHERRY-STONES

The number of cherry stones on the plate should be counted, while saying, for the first stone, "this year"; the second stone "next year", the third stone, "sometime", the fourth stone, "never". If the number of stones exceeds four, the incantation is repeated. The word or words occurring at the last stone are said to be a prophecy of your fate as regards marriage. In the same way the petals of a daisy may be plucked, while a similar incantation is uttered until the flower is stripped of all its petals.

~

A similar charm may be employed to discover whom you will wed. Instead of saying "this year" and so on, say "Tinker, tailor, soldier, sailor, rich man, poor man, beggar-man, thief", the designation of the last stone, it is declared, will be the rank or calling of your future husband. Another, but less familiar incantation, is "Army, navy, peerage, trade, doctor, divinity, law".

A Faithful or a Fickle Chap?

When young women would know if
their lovers are faithful, they put three
nuts upon the bars of the grates, naming
the nuts after the lovers. If a nut cracks
or jumps the lover will prove unfaithful;
if it begins to blaze or burn, he has a
regard for the person making the trial.
If two nuts named after the girl and
her lover, burn together they will
be married.

NUTMEG

Have a care; for if you carry a nutmeg in your pocket, you'll certainly be married to an old man.

Two Hazel Nuts

'Two Hazel-Nuts I threw into the flame,
And to each nut I gave a sweetheart's name.
This with the loudest bounce me sore amaz'd
That in the flame of brightest colour blaz'd
As blaz'd the nut so may thy passion grow,
For twas thy nut that did so brightly glow.'

FRUIT STONES

Plum jam tarts are made for single young women and meant to eat at wedding parties. The first tart a person eats is particularly noticed, for according to the number of plum stones found, so will years be before the person gets married.

LEMON PEEL

She who desires to be satisfied, whether she shall enjoy the man desired or no; let her take two lemon peels in the morning, and wear them all day under the arm pits. Then at night let her rub the four posts of the bed with them: which done, in your sleep he will seem to come and present you with a couple of lemons; but if not, there is no hope.

MASHED POTATOES

Mashed potatoes are the correct dish for Hallowe'en and they also offer us a method of divining which member of the company will be the first to wed. Into the heap of mashed potatoes a ring, a threepenny-bit, a button, a heart-shaped charm, a shell and a key are inserted. Then all the lights in the room are turned out, and each guest, armed with a spoon or fork, endeavours to find the hidden charms. The one who finds the ring will marry first; the threepenny-bit signifies wealth; the button, bachelorhood or spinsterhood; the heart, passionate love; the shell, long journeys; the key, great success and power.

BACON CURL

If the rashers of bacon curl up when frying, then a new lover is about to turn up for some one or other of the females in the house.

THE PEA-POD

Take a pea-pod in which there are nine peas and suspend it over the doorway by means of a white thread. If the next person who enters by the same door is not a member of the family and is a bachelor or spinster, then your wedding will take place in not more than a year's time.

FRIED PEAS

On Passion Sunday fried peas are served up on a dish. Every one is furnished with a spoon; they help themselves in

regular succession and whoever gets the
last will be the first to be married.

BEAN IN A PEA POD
A custom in the North ... a bean, shell
and all, is put into one of the pea-pods,
whosoever gets this bean is to be married
first.

TO REVEAL THE FORTUNE OF A
FUTURE HUSBAND
Take a walnut, a hazel-nut and nutmeg,
grate them together and mix them with
butter and sugar and make them up into
small pills, of which exactly nine must be
taken on going to bed; and according to
your dreams, so will be the state of the
person you will marry. If a gentleman,
of riches; if a clergyman, of white linen;
if a lawyer, of darkness; if a tradesman,
of odd noises and tumults; if a soldier or

sailor, of thunder and lightning; if a
servant, rain.

SALT HERRING
Take as many herrings as there are
persons (servants generally perform these
feats in company), throw them into the
fire and roast them very dry, then eat
them, skin, bones, and all, go back-
wards-way to bed, each and all, and the
man who is to be the sweetheart of
anyone, will bring the one water in her
dreams.

A raw herring, swallowed bones and all
... is very provocative of dreams ..
Swains sometimes adopt this plan to get
a glimpse of their future wives!

SALT IN EGG

A magical receipt to know whom one
shall marry. Egges roasted hard, and the
yelke taken out and salt put in its sted,
filled up; to be eaten fasting without
supper, when one goes to bed.

WHITE OF EGG

Take a glass and half fill it with water.
Into this is thrown the white of an egg.
Then leave the receptacle to stand for a
few minutes upon a window sill exposed
to the sun's rays. The form the contents
are then supposed to assume, as they
float upon the water, represents the
trade of the prospective husband.

COFFEE AND TEA

The small white circles floating on a cup of coffee signify the number of warm affectionate kisses which your sweetheart is prepared to give you. If you see them floating on a cup of tea, it signifies that your lover will, at no distant date, be possessed of a considerable amount of wealth.

WISHBONE OR MERRY-THOUGHT

One version of the old custom of pulling the wishbone or the merry-thought of cooked foul is as follows: the skip-jack of a goose is always preserved, and the younger members of the family, or the servants, break it, by one taking hold of each end. The one retaining the longest piece will be the first to be married.

St Agnes' Day - January 21st
St Valentine's Day - February 14th
St Dunstan's Day - May 19th
St Thomas' Day - December 23rd

The Calendar

To sneeze on Sunday
Before you break your fast,
You'll see your true love
Before a week is past

Cut your nails on Saturday
Your lover will come on the Sabbath

Anyone born on St Dunstan's Day must
not write a love letter on that day

NEW MOON

The first time you see the change of the
moon in the new year hold your hands
across, saying this three times:
'New moon, new moon,
I pray thee tell me
This night who my true love will be'
Then go to bed without any more
speaking that night and you will certainly dream of the person you are to marry.

NEW MOON

Upon seeing the new moon, if a young
man kisses the first maid he meets with,
(without speaking before!) he will receive
a small gift. In the same way, if a
maiden kisses the first young man she
meets on this occasion without speaking
she will receive a gift.

FIRST FULL MOON OF THE YEAR

At the first full moon of the year, place
your mirror by the window to reflect it.
Female, you gaze, and your sweetheart'll
lookey auver your shoulder, and you'll
see his face in the glass.

CHARMING THE MOON

At the new moon immediately after the
new year's day, go out in the evening
and stand over the spears of the gate or
stile and looking on the moon, repeat
the following lines:-

All hail to thee, moon! all hail to thee!
I pr'y thee, good moon, reveal to me
This night, who my truelove must be!

The party will then dream of her future
husband.

FIRST NEW MOON OF THE YEAR

When you first see the new moon in the
new year, take your stocking off from
one foot, and run to the next stile; when
you get there, between the treat toe and
the next, you will find a hair which will
be the colour of your lover's ...

NEW MOON

A young woman should borrow a man's
black silk handkerchief and hold it
between her and the first new moon of
the year - and recite:-
"New moon! New moon! I hail thee,
This night for my truelove to see:
But his apparel for every day;
That I tomorrow may him ken,
From among all other men."
...she should then retire to bed back-
wards without speaking another word to
anyone.

CHRISTMAS EVE

On Christmas Eve Lancashire lads and
lasses seek to choose themselves mates by
setting their marked onions in the
chimney. The first whose onion bursts
is the first to marry.

St Thomas' Eve

On St Thomas' Eve, it was the custom
among girls to procure a large red onion,
into which after peeling, they would
stick nine pins, and say:
'Good St Thomas do me right
Send me my true love this night
In his clothes and his array
Which he weareth every day.'
Eight pins were stuck around one in the
centre, to which was given the name of
the swain - and they were certain to
dream of the desired person.

Shrove Tuesday

A button, a ring and a sixpence, should
be put in a pancake, which is cut into
sections and distributed; and the finder
will be unmarried, married or rich
according to the article found.

VALENTINE ... FIRST PERSON SEEN
The belief is universal that if you are single, the first unmarried person you meet outside the house on Valentine's Day will exercise an important influence over your future destiny. Fortunately there is a simple way of evading the hand of fate, open to those who desire a greater freedom in their choice of partner in wedlock - at least, if they are willing to remain indoors till the expiration of the spell at twelve pm.

~

There is another kind of Valentine; which is the first young man or woman that chance throws in your way, in the street, or elsewhere on that day.

COCK AND HEN
ON ST VALENTINES MORNING.
In the early morn of St Valentine, young women would look through the keyhole of the house door. If they saw only a single object, or person, they would go alone all that year. If they saw two or more they would be sure to have a sweetheart, but if they saw a cock and a hen they might be quite certain of being married before the year was out.

DRAWING LOTS
On Valentine's Eve, the names of a select number of one sex, are by an equal number of the other put into some vessel; and after that, everyone draws a name, which is called their valentine and which is also looked upon as a good omen of their being man and wife.

ST VALENTINE'S EVE
Write your suitors' names upon bits of paper, rolled them up in clay, and put them into water: the first to rise up, will be your valentine.

"St Agnes' Day comes by and by
When pretty maids do fast to try
Their sweethearts in their dreams to see,
Or know who shall their husbands be."

THE ROW OF PINS
On the eve St. Agnes, that is to say on
the night before the 21st day of January,
take a row of pins, and pull them out
every one, one after the other. Then
stick a pin in your sleeve and you will
dream of the one you shall marry.

AGNES SWEET AND AGNES FAIR

A number of young lads and lasses meet
together on the Eve of St. Agnes, and at
the hour of twelve, one by one, go to a
certain corn-field and throw in some
grain, after which they pronounce -
"Agnes sweet, and Agnes fair,
Hither thither, now repair;
Bonny Agnes, let me see,
The lad who is to marry me."

"On sweet St Anna's (St. Agnes') night,
Feed them with a promised sight,
Some of husbands, some of lovers,
Which an empty dream discovers."

ROSEMARY AND THYME

On St. Agnes' Day, take a spring of
Rosemary and another of Thyme,
sprinkle them with urine thrice ... put

the Rosemary into one shoe and the
Thyme into another; place your shoes on
each side your bed-head and going to
bed, say ...
"St. Agnes, that's to lovers king,
Come ease the trouble of my mind."

You will dream of your lover.

MYRTLE
On Midsummer Eve let a girl take a
sprig of myrtle and lay it in her prayer
book upon the words of the marriage
service.
'Wilt thou have this man to be thy
wedded husband?'
Then let her close her book, put it under
her pillow, and sleep upon it. If her
lover will marry her the myrtle will be
gone in the morning.

SNAIL

On May Day Eve the young girls used to go into the fields and collect snails. One creature was placed on a dinner-plate covered pretty thickly with flour, and on the morning of May Day the marks made on the flour by the crawling of the snail were interpreted as the initials of the girl's future husband!

The Rose and Other Plants

The Rose
This beautiful flower has ever been one
of the most prominent love-charms.

THE RED ROSE

Pluck a full-blown red rose during the
month of June, not later than 7 o'clock
in the morning and place it in a white
envelope. Seal the envelope with wax
and make an impression on the wax with
the third finger of your left hand. Now
place the envelope under your pillow and
carefully note your dreams on the
following night. If you dream of water,
fields, flowers, mountains, glass, children, parents, organ music, silver, or the
moon, you will be married within a year.
If in your dreams you see giants, ani-
mals, birds, fishes, paper, a looking-glass
or the sun, you will wait five years for
your wedding. To dream of gold, bells,
reptiles, storms or soldiers is unlucky in
these circumstances, for it means that
you will probably remain a spinster.

THE ROSE CHARM

For a young lady who is 'in love' to
receive a full blown red rose from the
hand of her accepted lover, means that
he believes her love to be of the truest
and purest kind. For her to receive a red
rose when it is in bud indicates that her
lover esteems her love as the sweetest
thing upon earth. As the rose is the
most highly prized of all flowers, it is
deemed to be the greatest compliment
that can be paid to the young lady to
have one presented to her by a strange
young man. It means that he has the
highest opinion of her personal good
sense and attractive beauteous charms.

"If a red rose is given to you
It tells you of a heart that's true
One who in your beauty sees
Charms to set his heart at ease.

He will love you when far away,
From you his heart will never stray,
You will be his chief delight,
Though your fair face is out of sight."

A WHITE ROSE

A white rose given to a young lady
signifies that the gentleman giving it
esteems her love of the purest and most
spotless kind that can be found in the
innocent hearts of the gentle creatures of
his acquaintance:

"The white rose is an emblem pure
Of true, sweet love, that will endure
When other loves will fade away,
Or change, or die, or soon decay.

The sweet white rose, if given you
Portrays your lover always true.
Upon his vows you may rely
True as the sun shines from the sky."

ROSE IN PAPER

On Midsummer Day pluck a rose; fold it
up in paper, and put it by till Christmas
Day. On that day wear it at church; and
... the man who comes to take it from
you will be your husband.

A Damask Rose
If a lover presents a full-blown damask
rose to his lady-love, he is about to offer
her his heart and hand in marriage:
"The damask rose, given in full bloom,
Gives unto courtship's days their doom;
It heralds the happy day of days,
When hearts unite in wedlock's ways."

To See a Future Husband using Rose Water
On Midsummer's Eve just after sunset,
three, five or seven young women are to
go into a garden in which there is no
other person, and each to gather a sprig
of red sage. Then, going into a room by
themselves, set a stool in the middle of
the room, and on it a clean basin full of
rose water in which the sprigs of sage are
to be put, and, tying a line across the

room, on one side of the stool each
woman is to hang on it a clean chemise,
turned the wrong side outwards. Then
all are to sit in a row, on the opposite
side of the stool, as far distant as the
room will admit, not speaking a single
word the whole time, whatever they see,
and in a few minutes after twelve, each
one's future husband will take her sprig
out of the rose water and sprinkle her
shift with it.

HOLLY TWIG

Before retiring to rest, split a holly twig
and bind within the split part, a small
slip of paper, upon which you have
written the name of him you love best.
Place the twig under your pillow, and
you may dream of your fate.

NINE LEAVES

The leaves of the she Holly (smooth
edged) are alone deemed proper for
divination. These must be plucked, late
on a Friday in a three cornered handkerchief, nine of them must be selected,
tied with nine knots into the handkerchief and placed beneath the pillow.
Dreams of your future partner follow.

FLOWERS - IN PAIRS

Two flowers that have not blossomed are paired and put by themselves, as many pairs as there are sweethearts in the neighbourhood, as tall and short as the respective sweethearts are. The initials of their names are attached to the stamens, and they are arranged in order in the hayloft or stable, in perfect secrecy, except to those who manage and watch their secret growth. If, after ten days, any flower turns a contrary way, it indicates a want of affection; if any flower blossoms, it denotes early off-spring; if any flower wears a downcast appearance, sickness is indicated.

MYRTLE

Take from your bosom a sprig of myrtle,
which you must have worn there all day,
and fold it up in a piece of tissue paper,
then light up a small chaffing dish of
charcoal, and on it each maiden throw
nine hairs from her head, and you will
be sure to dream of your future husband.

MYRTLE - A SYMBOL OF LOVE

The Myrtle was both by the Greeks and
Romans, considered symbolic of love
The Roman bridegroom decked himself
with Myrtle on his bridal day ... with the
Jews, the Myrtle is a symbol of peace,
and ... Jewish maidens were wont to be
decked with a bridal wreath of Myrtle.

RICH MAN POOR MAN

Young women pluck a large daisy, pull
off the petals one by one, repeating,
"Rich man, poor man, farmer, plough-
man, thief", fancying that the one which
came to be named at plucking the last
petal would be her husband.

HEMP SEED

Carry the seed in your apron and with
your right hand throw it over your left
shoulder, saying thus,
"Hemp-seed I sow, hemp-seed I sow
And he that be my true love
Come after me and mow."
And at the ninth time expect to see the
figure of him you are to wed, or else hear
a bell.

To Dream Of Your Sweetheart

Take five bay leaves, attach four of them
on the four corners of your pillow, and
the fifth to the middle. If that night you
dream of your sweetheart, you will be
wed before the year is out.

Take two bay leaves, sprinkle them with
rose water; the evening of this day, lay
them across under your pillow, when
you go to bed putting on a clean shift,
and turning it wrong side outwards; and
lying down, say...

'Good valentine be kind to me,
In dreams let me my true love see.'

So crossing your legs, go to sleep ... you
will see in a dream the party you are to
marry.

LOVELACES

You must gather four long blades of
grass, called lovelaces
and hold them in your hand. Then tie
them in four knots, two at each end,
saying ...
"If you love me cling all round me,
If you hate me fall off quite.
If you neither love nor hate
Come in two at last."
If the grasses form a ring, he is constant:
if all the knots come undone, he hates
you; If they come in two pieces, he is
indifferent.

WILL MY LOVER BE TRUE-HEARTED?

The lover takes a blade of grass in his mouth, and, turning to the east and the west, says:

> "When the sun goes up
> Shall my love be by me
> Where the sun goes down,
> There, by her, I'll be."

Then the blade of grass is cut into pieces and mingled with some food which the girl must eat, and if she swallows the least bit of grass, she will be moved to love, and be true hearted.

The Ribwort Magic

Ribwort heads are plucked and concealed in the bosom; if they blow (put out stamens) one's lover is thinking of the experimenter.

Gather two blooming spikes of the ribwort plantain; one spike to represent the lad, the other the lass. All vestige of bloom must be rubbed off them and the pair wrapped in a dock leaf and laid beneath a stone. If on the following morning the spikes have bloomed again, then, according to the popular belief, there will be "Aye love between them twae".

LAUREL LEAF

Here is a country receipt for discovering
whether a lover is faithful or not. Take a
laurel leaf, scratch his name on it, or the
initials, and put in in the bosom of your
dress. If it turns brown, he is true; if
not, he'll deceive you.

KNAPWEED
They pull the little blossom threads
From out the knotweed's button heads
And put the husk, with many a smile
In their white bosoms for a while
Then, if they guess aright the swain
Their loves' sweet fancies try to gain
'Tis said, that ere it lies an hour
'Twill blossom out with second flower.

DANDELION OR HAWKWEED SEEDS
The flower stalk must be plucked
carefully, so as not to injure the globe of
seeds and you are then to blow off the
seeds so many puffs to blow every seed
clean off, so many years it will be before
you are married.

Love me Love me not

The down heads of dandelion,
hawkweed and goatsbeard are blown and
the words "Love me, love me not,"
repeated, and prognostications drawn
from the number of seeds left.

Four-leaf Clover

If you find a four-leaf clover, place it in
your right shoe and the next bachelor of
your acquaintance you meet will become
your husband.

White heather, even-ash, or four-leaf
clover,
You'll get good luck and see your love
'fore the day is over.

Two-leaf Clover
Put a two-leaf clover in your right shoe.
The first young man you meet, in field,
street or lane, you'll have him or one of
his name.

Four-leaf Clover
Let a young woman pin a four-leaved
clover over the door and the first
unmarried man who comes in the door
will be the one she is to marry.

Ivy Leaf
Pick an ivy leaf unobserved and repeat:

"Ivy, ivy, I pluck thee,
In my bosom I lay thee,
The first young man who speaks to me
Shall surely my true lover be."

To Dream of the Man You Love

One way to dream of the man you love
and are likely to marry:
On retiring to rest, get an ivy leaf (but
you must not look at it!), put it under
your pillow, thinking at the same time of
the one you love, and your dreams will
be of him.

Nine Sage Leaves

On All Saint's Eve, a young woman
must go out into the garden alone at
midnight and while the clock strikes
twelve she must pluck nine sage-leaves,
one on every stroke up to the ninth.
Then, if she is destined to be married,
she will see the face of her future
husband.

WATCHING THE FERN

On the night the tiny fern-seed, (which grows on the back of the leaf), is supposed to be ripe, good fortune will follow the lover who can catch some of the seed as it falls, by holding under it a bag or a white napkin - on no account must it be touched by the hands. This magic seed, which must be gathered alone and at midnight, will ensure success in love and bring wealth.

Sometimes the seed was called the "wish-seed" and if carried about in the pocket would ensure a happy courtship. Other magic plants to be gathered were the St John's Wort, or Orpine plant and the Mugwort.

ORPINE

The sprig or orpine should be set
upright in a lump of clay laid upon a
piece of slate, and according to the
direction in which the stalk was found
the following morning so would the
maiden's love affairs progress. If the
stalk inclined to the right the lover was
loyal and true, if it bent to the left he
was false.

MISTLETOE CHARM

If a bush of mistletoe is hung in the hall,
with the charm attached to it, it is said
that the maid who was not kissed under
it at Christmas, would not be married
that year.

MISTLETOE
THE KISSING PRIVILEGE

Mistletoe is hung in houses at Christmas; and the young men have the privilege of kissing the girls under it, plucking each time a berry from the bush. When the berries are all gone, the privilege ceases.

MAGPIE DREAM

If you should see two magpies together,
expect to hear something to your
advantage - a proposal of marriage if
single or a legacy of money bequeathed
to you. Should the magpie fly past you
together to your right hand, your own
marriage, or the marriage of someone
close to you will occur shortly.

MAGPIE RHYME

'One for anger, Two for mirth
Three for a wedding, Four for a birth
Five for rich, Six for poor,
Seven for a bitch, Eight for a whore
Nine for a burying, Ten for a dance
Eleven for England, Twelve for France.'

BLACKBIRDS

Although blackbirds are considered
unlucky to lovers, yet, if a young maiden
who has received the vows and promises
of love from her sweetheart the night
before on looking from her chamber
window, sees one, or hears one sing
before she partakes of breakfast, it is a
sure indication that the protestations of
her lover are all that the heart can
deserve; he will be faithful and sincere in
his attachments.

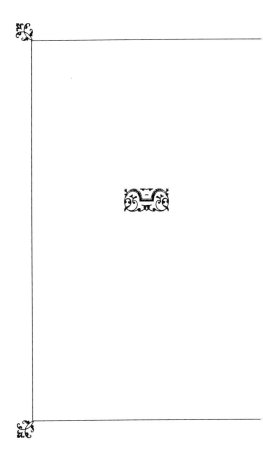

HOUSEHOLD TALES

A man should get possession of a
girl's garters, weaving them into a
true lover's knot and saying over
them words of hope and love.
Then he should keep them under
his shirt, next to his heart, till he goes
to bed, when he places them under
the bolster.
If the test be successful the vision of
his future wife appears to him in the
night.

PATCHWORK QUILT
If a lady completes one of these without
assistance, she will never be married.

BEDMAKING
Maidservants consider it very unlucky to
turn a feather bed on a Sunday; if you do
it, 'You're sure to lose your sweetheart.'

PINS ACROSS THE CANDLE
Those desirous to see their lovers should
stick two pins across through the candle
- taking care that the pins pass through
the wick. Whilst doing this they should
recite:
"It's not this candle alone I stick
But A B's heart I mean to prick
Whether he be asleep or awake
I'd have him come to me and speak."

CANDLE WICK
If any young girl sees a speck on the candle wick when it is burning she may be sure that her sweetheart is thinking of her and will pay her a visit shortly.

DON'T SPLASH!
If you splash yourself very much when you wash clothes you will have a drunken husband!

FIRE POKING
If you stir up the fire so that the kettle may boil and the fire burn brightly, some may say "your spark's bright tonight" - meaning that your lover is in a good humour.

THIS KNOT I KNIT

To see a future spouse in a dream: the
party inquiring must lie in a different
county from that in which she normally
resides and on going to bed, must knit
the left garter about the right-legged
stocking, letting the other garter and
stocking alone; rehearsing the following
verse, at every comma knit a knot:-

'This knot I knit, to know the thing I
know not yet,
That I may see the man that shall my
husband be,
How he goes, and what he wears,
And what he does all days and years.'

Accordingly, in a dream he will appear,
with the insignia of his trade
or profession.

A GARTER ROUND THE BEDPOST

Whenever I go to lie in a strange bed, I
always tie my garter nine times round
the bed-post and knit nine knots in it
and say to myself,

"This knot I knit, this knot I tie,
To see my love as he goes by,
In his apparel and array
As he walks in every day."

Knife Spinning

To find out whether your husband will have light hair or dark hair, take a table-knife with a white shaft and spin it round on the table. If it stops with the blade towards you your husband will be a dark haired man; If with the shaft, he will be a light haired man.

Stockings

On a Friday night before getting into bed, servant girls would draw their left stocking into the right, saying:
"This is the blessed Friday night;
I draw my left stocking into my right,
To dream of the living, not of the dead,
To dream of the young man I am to wed."
After this she would not speak again that night.

Turning the Smock

Three or four of you .... must take your
smocks and dip them in fair water, then
turn the wrong sides outwards, and hang
them on the chairs before the fire. Have
by you a vessel with drink in it and lay
some salt in another beside the fire, and
be sure not to speak whatever you see or
hear. In a little time the likeness of
those persons you shall marry will come
and turn your smocks, and drink to you;
now if there be any of you that will
never marry, they will hear a bell.

"Those dressed in blue
Have lovers true
In green and white
Forsaken quite."

A Stocking Spell

Girls should pin their woollen stockings
to the wall, and repeat :
"I hang my stockings on the wall,
Hoping my true love for to call;
May he neither rest, sleep, nor happy be,
Until he comes to speak to me."

Who Pulls My Yarn?

Young females go out at midnight and
cast a ball of yarn into a lime-kiln, whilst
holding on by a thread. If the girl winds
on, and if nothing holds the yarn, it is a
sign that the winder will die unmarried.
If she feel it pulled from her, she asks:
"Who pulls my yarn?" when it is
supposed her future husband will give
his name, or appear to her.

A Crooked Sixpence

A crooked sixpence is cut in twain, one
half is kept by the man, the other by the
maid, and so long as the portion is
retained will love remain true and
constant.

Blade-Bone Spell

A shoulder of mutton with nine holes
bored in the blade bone, is put under the
pillow to dream on. At the same time
the shoes of the experimenting damsel
are placed at the foot of the bed in the
shape of a letter T. The damsel may
then dream of her lover in his every-day
clothes.

ONIONS

If a lover does not come often enough,
he may be brought by roasting an onion
which has been stuck full of ounce pins.
(They must not have been through
paper) The pins are to prick his heart.

TO GET YOUR HEART'S DESIRE

Take an onion, a tulip or any root of any
kind: (ie a bulbous root) and plant it in a
clean pot never used before; and while
you plant it, repeat the name of whom
you love, and every day, morning and
evening, say over it;
"As this root grows
And as this blossom blows
May her heart be
Turned unto me!"
And it will come to pass that every day
the one whom you love will be more

inclined to you, till you get your heart's desire.

THE WITCHES CHAIN

Three young women must join in making a chain, a yard long, of vines, juniper and mistletoe berries and at the end of every link put an oak acorn. Exactly before midnight, they assemble in a room by themselves where no one can disturb them. A window must be left open, the key taken out of the keyhole and hung over the chimney piece. Have a good fire and place in the midst of it a long thinnish log of wood well sprinkled with oil, salt and fresh mould. Then wrap the chain around it, each young woman having an equal share in the business. Then sit down, and on your left knee, let each fair one have a prayer book opened at the matrimonial service. Just as the last acorn is burnt the future husband will cross the room. Each will see her own proper spouse, but he will be invisible to the rest of the wakeful virgins. Go to bed and you will have remarkable dreams. This must be done only on a Wednesday and Friday night.

HAIR, THROWN INTO THE FIRE

To discover who is fated to be their future partner ... two girls sit together in a room from twelve till one o' clock in the morning unknown to anyone. They then take as many hairs from their heads as they are years old. Immediately on the clock striking one, they put each hair separately on the fire saying;

'I offer this my sacrifice
To him most precious in my eyes
I charge thee now come forth to me
That I this minute thee may see.'

The spirit of her future husband will appear - each seeing her own, and not her friend's fiancee.

STREAKS IN ASHES

Make smooth the ashes on the hearth, and then make streaks on it with a stick. Each streak should signify privately to her that makes it, a certain unmarried man. In this way it is possible to know whom they should marry.

THE PRESENT OF SCISSORS

It is considered unlucky to accept scissors or other cutlery from lovers, lest it should sever their love.

THREE SAUCERS

Take three saucers. One is filled with clear water, another with ink or muddy water, while the third is left empty. A woman who wishes to know her fortune is blind-folded and led towards the table with her left hand outstretched. She is then told to touch one of the saucers. Should she touch the saucer containing the clear water, she will soon be married to a handsome man; should she touch the saucer containing the ink or muddy water her future husband will be a widower; if she should touch the empty saucer, she is unlikely to marry at all.

LAST DRINK

The last glass of wine or spirits drained from the last bottle of new year's eve or day is called the "lucky glass". It brings good fortune for whoever comes in for it and if an unmarried person drinks it, he will be the first to marry amongst the company.

LADYBIRD

"This lady-fly I take from off the grass
Whose spotted back might scarlet red
surpass
Fly, lady-bird, north, south, or east or
west,
Fly where the man is found that I love
best.
He leaves my hand, see, to the west he's
flown,
To call my truelove from the faithless
town."

The young woman who takes the last
piece of bread from the plate will marry
a rich man.

TAKE A RIDDLE
Sometimes girls take a riddle, and collect
a quantity of thrashed grain, which they
winnow, believing they shall see a future
spouse before their work is ended.

HOW MANY CHILDREN
Pull a stalk of oats, and according to the
number of grains upon the stalk, the
puller will have a corresponding number
of children.
It should also be observed that it is
essential to a maiden's good name that
her stalk should have the top grain
attached to it!

BALL

A girl sent a ball against the tree and drove it back again as often as she could, saying the following rhymes, in order to divine her matrimonial future:

'Keppy ball, keppy ball, Coban tree
Come down the long loanin' and tell to me,
The form and the features, the speech and degree
Of the man that is my true love to be ...
How many years old am I to be
One, a maiden, two a wife,
Three a maiden, four a wife ... etc.'

ASH TREE

The leaf of an ash which has an even
number of divisions on each side, which
is very difficult to obtain, is pulled with
the following rhyme:
'Even ash, I pull thee off the tree
The first young man that I do meet
My lover he shall be.'

It is then placed in the left shoe.

TO WIN THE LOVE OF A MAID

Get some willow-knots, cut one of them,
and put it into thy mouth and say:-
"I eat thy luck
I drink thy luck
Give me that luck of thine."

Old Irish Love Charm

A woman must hand to her beloved a
cup of water; while saying softly:
'You for me, and I for ye,
I for you, and you for me,
And for no one other;
Your face to mine, and your heart to me,
Your hand to me, and your head to be
Turned away from all others.'

Seven Years' Love

Would you like to make a temporary
conquest of an indifferent acquaintance?
Give him a spray of 'seven years' love',
which is the double-flowered yarrow.
He will love you in and out of season,
for seven years to the day, but not an
hour after.

WHO WILL BE THE FIRST TO MARRY?
Four cups of the same size are set upon a
circular table. In one of the cups there is
placed a ring, in another a sixpenny-
piece and in another a sprig of orange-
blossom or a piece of heather, while the
last cup remains empty. Those who
wish to take part in the test are blind-
folded and must walk slowly three times
round the table and then touch one of
the cups on it.

The first person to touch the cup
containing the orange-blossom or
heather will be the first to wed
anyone selecting the cup with the coin
will never know want;
the cup with the rings represents
devoted love;
while the empty cup suggests a single
life.

CARDS AND MATRIMONY

Let three, five and seven women stand in a circle, and draw a card out of a bag. She who gets the highest card will be the first to be married, whether she be at the present time maid, wife or widow; and she who has the lowest has the longest time to stay until the wedding day. She who draws the ace of spades will never bear the name of wife, and she who has the nine of hearts in this trial will have one lover too many, to her sorrow!

BARLEY

Take three stalks of barley from the
fields as the clock strikes the hour of
midnight, when they are ripe and first
barely ready for the sickle; wrap them
carefully in the last new pocket handkerchief which your lover made you a
present of; be careful not to crush or
break the stalks and ears then lay them
under your pillow and when you retire
to rest, just before going to sleep, repeat
the following lines three times over:
'Ripe ears of barley tell me true
How long my lover will renew
His promises before he'll wed
And take me to his marriage bed.'

At 9.00am unwrap the handkerchief
carefully. If all the ears have remained
on the stalks, your lover will ask your

hand in marriage during the next twelve
months; but if any of the ears which
were on the stalks have been separated,
count them, for they represent the
number of years you will be courted
before your lover will make you his wife.

Two Spoons

Two spoons in a cup or basin are the
sign of a wedding before the year is out,
some say the wedding of the person
who inadvertently added the second
spoon.

If two spoons are accidentally handed to
anyone with a cup of tea, he or she will
be married twice.

CUCKOO

When you hear the cuckoo for the first time, on taking off your left shoe you will find a hair of precisely the same colour as the hair of the person you are to be married to.

~

Those who are unmarried can count the number of years before they are wed, by the number of cuckoo's notes they count in the spring.
The number of times the cuckoo calls usually is accepted as the number of years.

A GREAT CHARM FOR LOVE
The hair from off the belly of a goat, tied
into knots and concealed in the roof of
the house of the beloved, will produce
furious love, whereby the maiden will
not be able to resist the entreaties of her
lover, but will be so enchanted with him
that marriage will soon take place.

BLACK CAT
The cat is often the object of supersti-
tion and it is said that:

"Whenever the cat of the house is black,
The lasses of lovers will have no lack."

ON RECEIPT OF A LOVE LETTER

On receipt of a love letter that contains
any particular declaration, lay it wide
open, then fold it in nine folds, pin it
next to your heart, and thus wear it till
bed time.

Then place it in your left hand glove,
and lay it under your head. If you dream
of gold, diamonds or any other costly
gems, your lover is true, and means what
he says; if of white linen, you will lose
him; if of his saluting you, he is at
present false, and means not what he
professes, but only to draw you into a
snare.

BE KIND TO CATS
Be kind to cats, you who desire sweet-tempered husbands when you marry. If you use them ill, it will rain and thunder at your wedding.

Index

Who Will Your Sweetheart Be?
Counting The Pips
Apple Charms
The Wish Of Your Heart
Pippins On The Tongs
Names In Bread
Bread And Cheese
Bread - Cutting or Pricking
Corn In The Circle
Cabbage Stalk
The Flower Of The Well
Wedding-Cake
Dumb Cake
A Wedding Ring Or A Sixpence
Dreaming Bread
Groaning Cheese
The Cherry Stone
A Faithful Or A Fickle Chap?
Nutmeg
Two Hazel Nuts
Fruit Stones
Lemon Peel
Mashed Potatoes
Bacon Curl
The Pea-Pod
Fried Peas
Bean In A Pea Pod
The Fortune Of A Future Husband

Salt Herring
Salt In Egg
White Of Egg
Coffee And Tea
The Calendar
Moon Charms
Christmas Eve
St. Thomas' Eve
Valentine - First Person Seen
Cock And Hen On St Valentines Morning
Drawing Lots
St Valentine's Eve
The Row Of Pins
Agnes Sweet And Agnes Fair
Rosemary And Thyme
Myrtle
Snail
The Red Rose
The Rose Charm
A White Rose
Rose In Paper
A Damask Rose
To See A Future Husband Using Rose Water
Holly Twig
Nine Leaves
Flowers - in Pairs
Myrtle
Myrtle - A Symbol Of Love
Rich Man Poor Man
To Dream Of Your Sweetheart

Lovelaces
Will My Lover Be True-Hearted?
The Ribwort Magic
Laurel Leaf
Knapweed
Dandelion Or Hawkweed Seeds
Love Me Love Me Not
Four-Leaf Clover
Two-Leaf Clover
Four-Leaf Clover
Ivy Leaf
To Dream Of The Man You Love
Nine Sage Leaves
Watching The Fern
Orpine
Mistletoe Charm
Mistletoe The Kissing Privilege
Magpie Dream
Magpie Rhyme
Blackbirds
Patchwork Quilt
Bedmaking
Pins Across The Candle
Candle Wick
Don't Splash!
Fire Poking
The Knot I Knit
A Garter Round The Bedpost
Knife Spinning
Stockings

Turning The Smock
A Stocking Spell
Who Pulls My Yarn?
A Crooked Sixpence
Blade-Bone Spell
Onions
To Get Your Heart's Desire
The Witches Charm
Hair, Thrown Into The Fire
Streaks In Ashes
The Present Of Scissors
Three Saucers
Last Drink
Ladybird
Take A Riddle
How Many Children
Ball
Ash Tree
To Win The Love Of A Maid
Old Irish Love Charm
Seven Years' Love
Who Will Be The First To Marry?
Cards And Matrimony
Barley
Two Spoons
Cuckoo
A Great Charm For Love
Black Cat
On Receipt Of A Love Letter
Be Kind To Cats